FIONA FRENCH won the 1986 Kate Greenaway Medal
for her book *Snow White in New York*. In 1992, *Anancy and Mr Dry-Bone*, her first book for
Frances Lincoln, which she also wrote, was selected for Children's Books of the Year
and won the Sheffield Book Award. *Pepi and the Secret Names*, written by Jill Paton Walsh, was
described by *Child Education* as "stunning, a superb example of Fiona French at her very best,"
en as one of their Best Story Books of 1994. *Little Inchkin, Lord of the Animals, Jamil's Clever Cat*
Dunbar's *The Glass Garden*, published during the 1990s, all reflect Fiona's wide-ranging
e styles. *Easter* is the second title in Fiona's series of illuminated Biblical texts.
n *Bethlehem*, which is a stained glass re-creation of the Nativity, with words taken
Authorized King James Version of the New Testament. Her latest title
in the series is *Paradise*, a stunning illustrated version
of the creation story taken from Genesis.

For my father, Robert French,
and for Brian and Jennifer Chandler,
Les Hughes (in memory)
and for Mavis Hughes and Jane Hill

First published in Great Britain in 2002 by
Frances Lincoln Children's Books, 4 Torriano Mews, Torriano Avenue, London NW5 2RZ
www.franceslincoln.com

First paperback edition published in 2004

British Library Cataloguing in Publication Data
available on request

ISBN 1-84507-013-5
Set in Hadriano Light

Printed in Singapore
1 3 5 7 9 8 6 4 2

EASTER

FIONA FRENCH

With words from the Authorized Version of the
KING JAMES BIBLE

FRANCES LINCOLN

When they heard that Jesus was coming to Jerusalem, people took branches of palm trees, and went forth to meet him, and cried, "Hosanna: Blessed is the King of Israel that cometh in the name of the Lord!"

Now when the even was come,
Jesus sat down with the twelve.
And as they did eat, Jesus took bread,
and blessed and brake it, and gave
to them and said, "Take, eat: this is
my body."

And he took the cup, and when he had given thanks he gave it to them: and they all drank of it.

Then cometh Jesus with them unto a place called Gethsemane. And Judas, one of the twelve, came, and with him a great multitude with swords and staves from the chief priests and elders of the people.

Now he that betrayed him gave
them a sign, saying, "Whomsoever
I shall kiss, that same is he: hold
him fast." And he came to Jesus
and said, "Hail, master", and
kissed him. Then they laid
hands on Jesus, and took him.

And as they came out, they found
a man of Cyrene, Simon by name:
him they compelled to bear Jesus' cross.
And they were come unto a place called
Golgotha, that is to say, a place of a skull.

And they crucified him.

When the even was come,
there came a rich man
of Arimathaea named Joseph,
who also himself was Jesus' disciple.
He went to Pilate and begged the body
of Jesus. And when Joseph had taken
the body, he wrapped it in a clean linen cloth
and laid it in his own new tomb, and he rolled
a great stone to the door of the sepulchre,
and departed.

Now upon the first day of the week, very early in the morning, Mary Magdalene and the other Mary came unto the sepulchre, and found the stone rolled away. They entered in, and found not the body of the Lord Jesus.

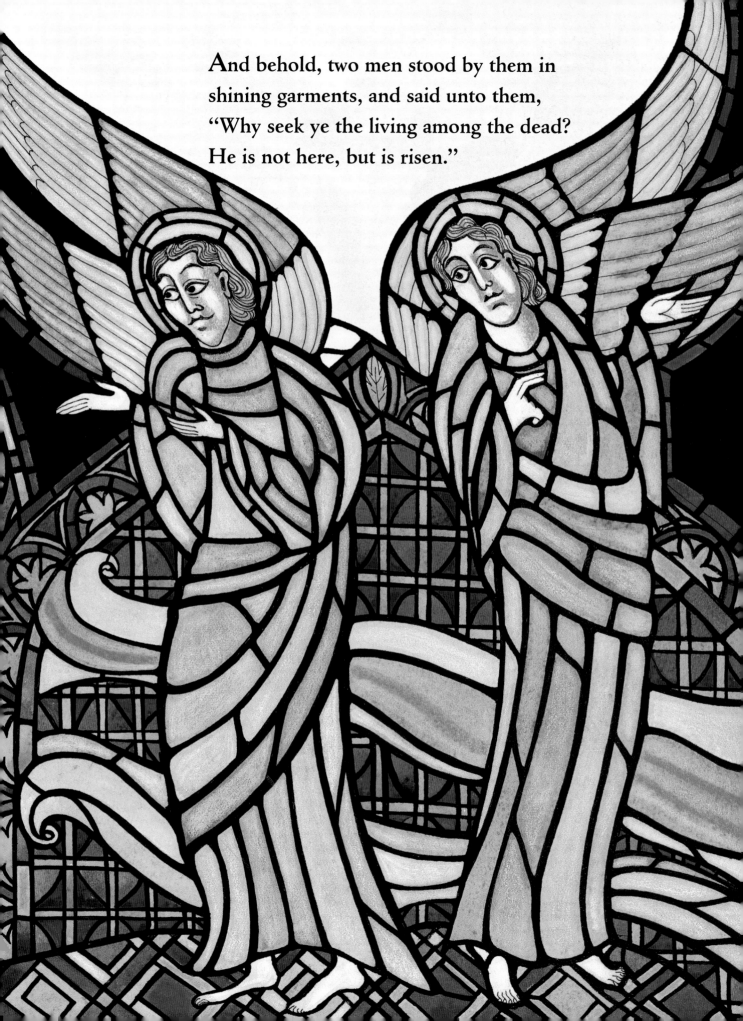

And behold, two men stood by them in shining garments, and said unto them, "Why seek ye the living among the dead? He is not here, but is risen."

Then the same day at evening, when the disciples were assembled, came Jesus and saith unto them, "Peace be unto you." But Thomas, one of the twelve, was not with them when Jesus came. The other disciples said unto him, "We have seen the Lord." But he said, "Except I shall see in his hands the print of the nails, and thrust my hand into his side, I will not believe."

After eight days
his disciples were within, and
Thomas with them: then came Jesus
and stood in the midst. Then saith he
to Thomas, "Behold my hands, and reach
hither thy hand and thrust it into my side,
and be not faithless, but believing."
And Thomas said, "My Lord and my God!"

Jesus shewed himself again to the disciples at the sea of Tiberias. He saith unto them, "Children, have ye any meat?" They answered him, "No." And he said, "Cast the net on the right side of the ship, and ye shall find." They cast therefore, and were not able to draw it for the multitude of fishes.

As soon then as they were
come to land, they saw a fire
of coals there, and fish laid
thereon, and bread. Jesus saith
unto them, "Come and dine."
And none of the disciples durst
ask him, "Who art thou?"
knowing that it was the Lord.

And he led them out as far as to Bethany, and he lifted up his hands and blessed them. And it came to pass, while he blessed them, he was parted from them and carried up into heaven. And they worshipped him, and returned to Jerusalem with great joy.

MORE TITLES FROM
FRANCES LINCOLN CHILDREN'S BOOKS

Bethlehem
FIONA FRENCH

Inspired by the stained glass windows of Ely Cathedral,
Fiona French illuminates the timeless beauty of the Christmas story in kaleidoscopic colour, with words
from the King James Bible. Beginning on the road to Bethlehem, scene by scene the pages
portray the wonderful events surrounding the birth of Jesus.

ISBN 0-7112-1576-6

Paradise
FIONA FRENCH

Twelve glorious tableaux portray the Old Testament story of the creation –
seven momentous days in which God creates the world: light and dark, sky and earth, fishes,
birds, animals and finally man and woman.

Fiona French's images – inspired by the organic lines of Art Nouveau and
Louis Comfort Tiffany's stained glass – combine with words taken from the Authorized King James
version of the Bible to bring the Book of Genesis into glowing perspective
for readers both young and old.

ISBN 1-84507-007-0

I Believe
PAULINE BAYNES

Pauline Baynes, the much-loved illustrator of C.S. Lewis's
The Chronicles of Narnia, has transformed the Nicene Creed into a joyous hymn to God.
Her breathtaking images of the sun, moon and stars, creatures great and small, death
and resurrection are based on a lifetime's passion for Anglo-Saxon and Persian manuscripts.
She brings them together here in a spirited affirmation
of faith to delight and inspire.

ISBN 0-7112-2120-0

Frances Lincoln titles are available from all good bookshops.
You can also buy books and find out more about your favourite titles, authors and illustrators
on our website: www.franceslincoln.com